Camdean School

363

Item no.   00289

KU-376-215

Safety Near Water

DOROTHY BALDWIN and CLAIRE LISTER

Safety First

Safety at School
Safety in the Countryside
Safety in the Home
Safety Near Water
Safety on the Road
Safety When Alone

Editor: Paul Humphrey

The Publishers would like to thank the Royal Society for the Prevention of Accidents (ROSPA) for their assistance with the text and pictures.

First published in 1987 by
Wayland (Publishers) Limited
61 Western Road, Hove
East Sussex, BN3 1JD, England

British Library Cataloguing in Publication Data
Baldwin, Dorothy
Safety near water. – (Safety first).
1. Aquatic sports – Safety measures –
Juvenile literature
I. Title   II. Lister, Claire   III. Series
363.1'4   GV770.6

ISBN 1–85210–082–6

Phototypeset by
Kalligraphics Limited, Redhill, Surrey
Printed and bound in Belgium by
Casterman S.A.

Contents

All words that appear
in **bold** are explained in the
glossary on page 31.

About this book

Do you like the seaside? Are you learning to swim? Water can be great fun. But it can be dangerous as well. You need to know the SAFETY rules so you can enjoy yourself. Make sure you know the dangers, and do not take risks.

Accidents happen when people forget about safety. This book will show you the main points to watch out for.

Swimming is good exercise and great fun, too, but you should never swim on your own without an adult.

At the seaside

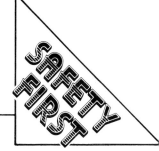

SAFETY FIRST

On a hot day the water looks lovely. You long to run straight in. Stop! Think! Look out for danger first! Never, ever, go swimming on your own. Go with a grown-up you know.

Tides and currents

The sea is much stronger than you are. Twice each day the **tide** rises up the beach and goes out again. **Currents** are strong movements of water under the surface. They pull the water along powerfully and

The sea may look calm but it is dangerous. Never swim there alone.

are strong enough to knock you over. Often, you cannot see currents from the shore. Nor can you tell if the tide is going in or out.

Look for the signs warning of danger:
- Red flag
- Noticeboard saying DANGER or NO SWIMMING

You must not go near the water if you see signs like these. Even paddling can be dangerous.

The beach

Check the beach. Is it pebbly or sandy? Pebble beaches are rougher than sandy ones. In the water, pebbles can be slippery with seaweed. You might lose your balance and fall over. The waves drag the pebbles to and fro quite roughly. Take extra care in the water. You may feel safer if you wear non-slip beach shoes.

Some beaches slope down to the sea. The slope of a beach is important. Can you wade gradually into the water? Or is there a steep slope? Even on a sandy beach, a steep slope can be dangerous. Never go down a steep slope into the sea on your own.

Some people like to get away from crowds. They look for empty beaches where there is nobody else around. But a deserted beach is NOT safe for children. Never, ever go alone or with a friend of your own age. You must have at least one adult with you.

Pollution

Unfortunately some beaches have become dirty. There may be tar or oil on the beach. This spoils your clothes and is difficult to get off your skin. Sometimes the pollution comes from **sewage** that is washed up on the beach. Do not play where there is any sign of sewage on the shore and keep away from all sewer pipes. Dogs, too, leave their mess on the beach. It is dangerous to play with any kind of mess, because it can make you ill.

Sometimes, dangerous chemicals are washed on to beaches by the tide. Do not touch any containers that have been washed up. If you see a danger sign on one, tell an adult. Do not touch it.

The bay

Bays are often worth exploring. They are full of exciting things. But you must remember that the sea has tides. They can come in and block your path. You could be trapped. Do not go climbing on rocks and cliffs. The tide could come in and you would be cut off. Strong waves or a sudden gust of wind could throw you into the water.

Do not go exploring on your own. Take a friend. Tell an adult where you are going and when you will be back. Take a watch. Do not go far out of sight. Make sure you are back on time.

Breakwaters and steps are often slippery. The water may be deeper than it looks. There could be strong currents swirling underneath. Rock pools are sometimes difficult to reach. Wear non-slip beach shoes. Take extra care where you put your feet.

Take care on steeply sloping beaches and near breakwaters.

Sea creatures

Most of the dangerous sea creatures, such as sharks and poisonous fish, live in the warmer seas of the world. There are also a few that you need to be careful of in cooler seas, too.

● Jellyfish

The Portuguese Man-of-War is a large jellyfish sometimes found in the seas around Europe. You may be able to see its pretty colours. But beware! The sting is very painful. In hot countries, jellyfish can be smaller and not easy to see. Make sure there are no jellyfish about before you go into the sea.

● Poisonous fish

Some spiny fish are poisonous to touch. One of these is the weever fish which lives in the sea around Britain and other parts of Europe. If you touch its sharp spines it can inject poison into your skin and give you a nasty wound.

So, watch out! Wear non-slip beach shoes to protect your feet. You can look at, but do not touch any strange sea creature.

● Sharks

Some sharks attack and kill people. Others do not. You cannot tell which is which. Never, ever go near the water if there are sharks about. Always check you are not in a shark-infested area before you go for a swim.

Here are some of the sea creatures to look out for while swimming.

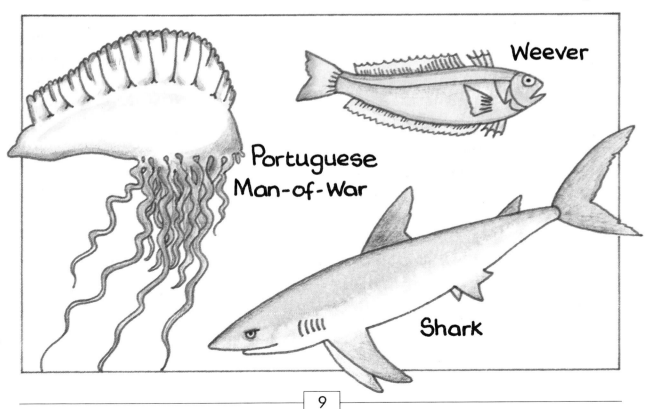

Weever

Portuguese Man-of-War

Shark

Swimming

Swimming is one of the best exercises for health. It builds up strong muscles, and keeps you very fit. If you cannot swim, go for lessons at your local public swimming baths. When you are at the seaside, remember these rules for non-swimmers:

- Stay close to an adult.
- Wear floats on your arms.
- Do not wade out too far.
- When the water reaches the tops of your legs, stop! That is far enough.
- Little children are not safe in the water at all.

If you cannot swim, you should always stay close to the shore, and near to an adult who can swim, while paddling in the sea.

Always swim along side the shoreline, not out to sea.

These are the safety rules for swimmers at the seaside:
● Always swim along beside the shoreline, not out to sea. Have a landmark in sight, so you keep your position. Stay in your depth. Keep checking you can touch the bottom with your feet.
● In your depth, you can stop for a rest when you feel tired. You can walk to the shore easily if something goes wrong.
● A colder patch of sea means you are in a current. Stay calm. Swim or walk steadily back to the safety of the shore.
● Do not stay too long in the water. Your muscles get tired before your brain does! Tired muscles can get **cramp**. Cramp is dangerous. Even strong swimmers get attacks, especially when the water is cold. If you get cramp, turn on your back and float. When the cramp goes,

use a different swimming stroke to prevent using the same muscles. Do not go swimming for at least two hours after a heavy meal because this can cause cramp.

At the pool

You can have great fun at a swimming pool. Playing in water helps to give you confidence, too. There are qualified people at swimming pools who can teach you to swim. Do not try to teach yourself.

First learn to stay afloat in water. Get someone to show you how to float. Learn how to 'tread' water, keeping yourself upright in deep water by 'treading' with your feet. Then you can learn more about swimming.

All these things will make it safer for you to play near water.

Remember these important points when you are at the pool:
● Do not run or play games near the edge of the pool. You could fall in and hurt yourself and others.
● Do not shout or shriek.
● Do not push people into the water.
● Make sure it is deep enough if you are going to jump in.
● Make sure you do not jump into the water where there are other people playing and swimming.
● Do not fool about in the water.
When you have learned to swim, take as many tests and gain as many badges as you can. They will help to make you safe in the water. But always remember that although you may be a good swimmer in the pool, this does not always mean you will be as good in cold, outdoor water.

The pool is often the best place to learn how to swim.

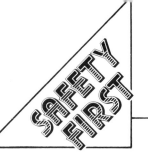

By rivers and canals

Rivers do not have tides, but some have strong currents. Many rivers have steep banks. Others have gentle slopes. Always play well back from the edge. If you do slip when you are running, then you only fall to the ground, not into the river.

These children should not be playing alone by the river. Why is this dangerous?

Paddling in rivers can be fun. But make sure you can get out easily and only paddle when the water is shallow. Never swim in a river. Rivers often have rushes, trailing roots and water-weeds growing in them. They could tangle around you.

Always remain well back from the edge while playing or picnicking on the river bank.

Picnics

A Sad Tale

Sarah and Jim were picnicking near the edge of the river bank. Sarah told a funny story. Jim started to laugh. He rolled over and over, and toppled into the river. As he fell, he choked on his sandwich. It became stuck in his throat.

'Swim to shore!' Sarah called. She knew Jim was a very good

Jim and Sarah were picnicking too close to the bank.

swimmer, so she didn't try to help him out.

Poor Jim! His airway was blocked. He couldn't breathe. He couldn't shout for help. The river was running swiftly and the water was dirty. Jim was carried away and out of sight.

Can you guess at the things which went wrong?

DO NOT FOOL AROUND NEAR WATER!

It is easy to roll down a steep slope. The children should have picnicked further back from the edge of the bank.

If you are eating and try to laugh and swallow at the same time, the food gets stuck in the airway. Choking is always serious. The blocked food must be coughed up at once. If coughing does not bring it up, the person should be given hard bangs on the back.

No matter how well someone can swim, it is not safe to take any risks near water. Turn to page 30 to read how Sarah could have helped Jim out.

Perhaps Sarah and Jim were too young to be on a picnic without adults. What do you think?

Canals and locks

Today, most canals are used by holidaymakers. Many people enjoy sailing in flat-bottomed boats called barges. The safety rules for barges are the same as for boats (see pages 19–22). Barges travel very slowly, however, so there is little danger from pitching and tossing. But you do need to be careful. Wear a **life-jacket**, remember to keep your hands inside the boat so that they do not get hurt, and look out for low bridges! You could get a nasty blow on the head and even be knocked into the water if you were not careful.

Some canals are very narrow. It is easy to fall down the gap between the canal bank and the barge and hurt yourself.

Locks control the level of water in the canals. They work like big doors, letting water in or keeping it out. It is exciting to watch them being opened and closed. But they can be very dangerous. There are many accidents at locks. People get excited and take terrible risks. On the next page, you will find four important points to remember when you are near canals or locks:

- The ground can be slippery. Make sure everyone stands well back.
- Hold small children very firmly by the hand.
- Boat hooks lying around cause accidents. Watch where you walk.
- Do not ask to climb on the machinery. It is dangerous.

It is exciting to watch a lock filling with water, but you should never play near canals or locks.

On a boat

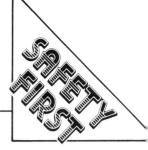

There are special safety rules for boats. Each boat is different, so each boat will have different safety rules. You will be told what they are when you go on board. Listen very carefully. You must learn them by heart and make sure you understand them.

Whether you are sailing at sea, or on the river, you must wear a life-jacket.

A life-jacket and a safety harness. The safety harness is used for attaching small children to a boat to prevent them from falling overboard.

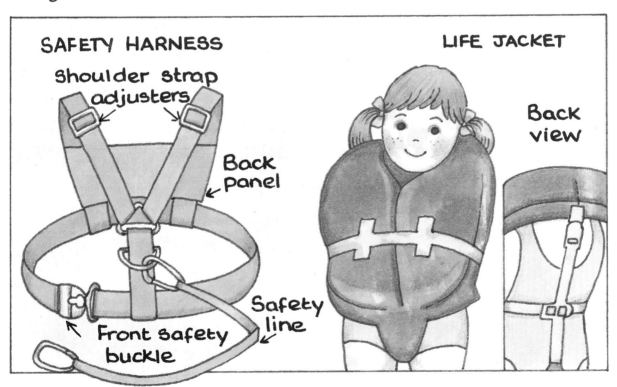

SAFETY HARNESS

Shoulder strap adjusters

Back panel

Front safety buckle

Safety line

LIFE JACKET

Back view

On water, accidents can happen very swiftly indeed. Good weather can suddenly change to bad. The wind can start to rise and quickly turn into a storm. Then high waves dash against the sides of the boat. Water pours in. Some small boats can easily fill with water and capsize. The people not wearing life-jackets have no time to find them!

The captain of a boat is responsible for everyone's safety. 'Captain's Orders' must be obeyed at once. You may be a passenger, or you may be working as a member of the crew. Whichever you are, you must obey all the safety rules the captain gives at all times.

These children should not have gone sailing without an adult. Luckily, they were wearing life-jackets when the dinghy capsized.

Some general rules

Never play around on a small boat. Keep your life-jacket on all the time. Do not take it off. Can you think of the reason why?

When the water is rough, the boat pitches and rolls. Do not run about. Hold on tight to a firm fixture. This will protect you from knocks and bruises.

Keep to the middle of the boat. Do not play near the sides. If there was a very strong pitch, you could be swept overboard. Do not take any risks.

Make sure that a grown-up straps small children into a safety harness. They must not be allowed to crawl near the side. Even on a

Sailing is great fun but remember, do not play around and always sit in the middle of the boat.

calm day, the rolling motion of the boat could tip them overboard. In rough weather, the captain may insist that all the crew are tied on with a rope. Why do you think this is?

You should always be especially careful when getting on or off a small sailing boat. You could easily fall into the water.

Water sports

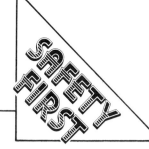

These people are having fun. But do you think anyone might be in danger? When you windsurf or water-ski, you have to concentrate on keeping your balance. You may be travelling very fast. It is not easy to watch out for people in the water. Without meaning to, you could cause a serious accident.

If you do water sports, keep away from places where people are swimming. When you go swimming, do not choose a place where water sports are going on. Some seaside places are very unsafe. They are crowded with people all trying to do different things at once. This is not safe. From the picture, find three people who could be in danger.

You should never practise water sports near to where people are swimming.

Air beds, rings and floats

Jane was playing with her air-bed. She stopped to watch the fisherman with his nets. When she turned back, she saw her air-bed had floated away. The tide had taken it right out to sea.

'Oh, my beautiful air-bed! I must get it back.' Without thinking, Jane swam after it. But the harder she swam, the further the air-bed floated out. Jane was frightened. Her legs hurt. She couldn't breathe properly.

'Help!' Jane called, and swallowed a mouthful of water. She realized she was far out at sea. 'I am drowning,' she thought.

Jane's mother looked up from her book. Where was Jane? She

Jane's air-bed floated out to sea. The tide carried it further out and she wanted to get it back.

searched the beach. She looked out to sea. Jane's mother shouted for the **lifeguard**. They both ran straight into the sea. 'Go back!' the lifeguard said. 'I will rescue her.'

Next term, Jane told the story in class. 'It was horrid. I almost drowned. It was my fault for being silly,' she said. 'I couldn't bear to lose my air-bed. I forgot about safety. I didn't stop to think. I might have lost my life as well.'

Not all stories end as happily as Jane's. Each year, children are drowned at sea because they go too far out on air-beds, rings and floats. What do you think Jane should have done when her air-bed floated out to sea?

The lifeguard had to rescue Jane because she had swum too far out and was too tired to get back to shore.

Fishing

Fishing is a popular sport. It is thrilling to feel a sudden tug on your line. Some people get over-excited when this happens. They scream and jump about. They forget the safety rules. They are so pleased to have caught a fish.

Fish hooks cause nasty accidents, especially those with barbs. If they catch under your skin, the barbs stop the hook being eased out. Keep all fishing hooks in a tightly-closed tin. Never leave them on the ground. Take care with rods and nets as well. Make sure no-one is close when you cast your line. When you have finished, fold the nets in a neat pile so that people do not trip over them.

Fishing is a great sport but remember the safety rules and be careful of fish hooks. They can prick you badly, especially those with barbs.

Ice skating

How graceful the skaters look! This outdoor ice rink is safe because it has been specially made for skating. But most frozen ponds and rivers are not at all safe. The ice is very thin. It could easily crack under your weight. If you fell into the icy water you would not be able to survive for very long.

It is difficult for anyone, even an adult, to know whether the ice on a pond is thick enough for skating.

To be safe, you should never skate on a frozen pond. Always go to a proper skating rink.

This ice rink has been specially designed. You should never skate on a frozen pond.

To the rescue!

This is a picture of an Air-Sea Rescue team. They are lifting a person out of the sea. It is dangerous to be in cold water. Cold water kills. If you do fall in, do not try to swim. Swimming takes away your body heat. Even very strong adults cannot swim far in the cold.

The person who is being rescued in this picture did not remember the safety rules. Make sure you never find yourself in this position.

In cold water, remember these rules:
- Stay calm. Breathe deeply and steadily.
- Do not try to swim.
- Cling to anything which floats.
- Look around you. Shout for help.

The coastguards are specially trained to rescue people in trouble in the water and to look out for dangers.

● Keep your head right out of the water — you lose half your body heat from your head.
● Keep as much of your body as possible out of the water as well.
● Do not take off any clothes, even your shoes or hat. They help you stay afloat and keep in your body heat.

Rescue!

If you see a person drowning, of course you want to help. But stop! Think of your own safety! You must not dive straight in. Drowning accidents happen each year because people rush to the rescue without thinking. If the waves are too high, or there are strong currents, the rescuers themselves get into difficulties. There is a risk they will lose their own lives.

● Look for help. There may be a lifeguard or other adult near. If you are with friends of your own age, tell one person to run for help.

● Throw a **lifebelt**, large ball or anything else that floats. A rope is very useful too. The person can cling on to it until further help arrives.

● Hold out a strong branch or stick to pull the person to shore. This can be dangerous on your own. Tell a friend to hold tightly to your waist or legs.

● Form a human chain in the water. Grasp each other's arms tightly. Make sure the person acting as 'anchor' holds on to something really strong on the land.

Train now for your Life-Saving Certificate. Practise how to save lives.

Here are three ways of helping someone who has fallen in the water: 1. Throw a lifebelt or anything else which floats. 2. Hold out a strong branch or stick for the person to hold on to. 3. Form a human chain to reach the person in the water. Never risk your own life.

Glossary

Breakwater A wall running down into the sea to break the force of the water.

Cramp Sudden tightening of the muscles, stopping you moving properly.

Current A fast-moving section of water.

Lifebelt A ring that floats on water. It is used to rescue people who have got into difficulties in the water.

Lifeguard A person who patrols a beach, river or swimming pool to make sure everyone is safe. Lifeguards rescue anyone in trouble in the water.

Life-jacket A safety jacket, filled with air, that helps people float in water until they are rescued.

Sewage Dirty water and waste carried down the drains from bathrooms, lavatories and kitchens. In some places sewage is dumped into the sea.

Tide The rise and fall of the sea level on a beach.

Books to Read

First Steps in First Aid by Ian Roy (Ladybird, 1981)
Water Safety by R. Birch (Ladybird, 1981)

Safety in the Countryside by Dorothy Baldwin and Claire Lister (Wayland, 1987)

Index

Picture acknowledgements
Sally & Richard Greenhill 8; Vision International *cover*, 4, 13, 14, 18, 22, 23, 26; Wayland Picture Library 29; Jenny Woodcock 15, Tim Woodcock 5, Zefa 27, 28. The artwork illustrations are by Colleen Payne.